R

by Iain Gray

Lang**Syne**
PUBLISHING
WRITING *to* REMEMBER

Lang**Syne**

PUBLISHING

WRITING *to* REMEMBER

79 Main Street, Newtongrange,
Midlothian EH22 4NA
Tel: 0131 344 0414   Fax: 0845 075 6085
E-mail: info@lang-syne.co.uk
www.langsyneshop.co.uk

Design by Dorothy Meikle
Printed by Martins the Printers, Berwick-upon-Tweed
© Lang Syne Publishers Ltd 2015

All rights reserved. No part of this publication may be reproduced, stored or introduced into a retrieval system, or transmitted in any form or by any means (electronic, mechanical, photocopying, recording or otherwise) without the prior written permission of Lang Syne Publishers Ltd.

ISBN 978-1-85217-644-0

Robinson

MOTTOES include:
Faithful
(and)
Faith is everything.

CRESTS include:
A gold stag, or buck,
emerging from a crown.

NAME variations include:
Robens
Robeson
Robbinson
Robbison
Robins
Robison
Robyns
Robson

Chapter one:

The origins of popular surnames

by George Forbes and Iain Gray

If you don't know where you came from, you won't know where you're going **is a frequently quoted observation and one that has a particular resonance today when there has been a marked upsurge in interest in genealogy, with increasing numbers of people curious to trace their family roots.**

Main sources for genealogical research include census returns and official records of births, marriages and deaths – and the key to unlocking the detail they contain is obviously a family surname, one that has been 'inherited' and passed from generation to generation.

No matter our station in life, we all have a surname – but it was not until about the middle of the fourteenth century that the practice of being identified by a particular surname became commonly established throughout the British Isles.

Previous to this, it was normal for a person to be identified through the use of only a forename.

But as population gradually increased and there were many more people with the same forename, surnames were adopted to distinguish one person, or community, from another.

Many common English surnames are patronymic in origin, meaning they stem from the forename of one's father – with 'Johnson,' for example, indicating 'son of John.'

It was the Normans, in the wake of their eleventh century conquest of Anglo-Saxon England, a pivotal moment in the nation's history, who first brought surnames into usage – although it was a gradual process.

For the Normans, these were names initially based on the title of their estates, local villages and chateaux in France to distinguish and identify these landholdings.

Such grand descriptions also helped enhance the prestige of these warlords and generally glorify their lofty positions high above the humble serfs slaving away below in the pecking order who had only single names, often with Biblical connotations as in Pierre and Jacques.

The only descriptive distinctions among the peasantry concerned their occupations, like 'Pierre the swineherd' or 'Jacques the ferryman.'

Roots of surnames that came into usage in England not only included Norman-French, but also Old French, Old Norse, Old English, Middle English, German, Latin, Greek, Hebrew and the Gaelic languages of the Celts.

The Normans themselves were originally Vikings, or 'Northmen', who raided, colonised and eventually settled down around the French coastline.

The had sailed up the Seine in their longboats in 900AD under their ferocious leader Rollo and ruled the roost in north eastern France before sailing over to conquer England in 1066 under Duke William of Normandy – better known to posterity as William the Conqueror, or King William I of England.

Granted lands in the newly-conquered England, some of their descendants later acquired territories in Wales, Scotland and Ireland – taking not only their own surnames, but also the practice of adopting a surname, with them.

But it was in England where Norman rule and custom first impacted, particularly in relation to the adoption of surnames.

This is reflected in the famous *Domesday Book*, a massive survey of much of England and Wales, ordered by William I, to determine who owned what, what it was worth and therefore how much they were liable to pay in taxes to the voracious Royal Exchequer.

Completed in 1086 and now held in the National Archives in Kew, London, 'Domesday' was an Old English word meaning 'Day of Judgement.'

This was because, in the words of one contemporary chronicler, "its decisions, like those of the Last Judgement, are unalterable."

It had been a requirement of all those English landholders – from the richest to the poorest – that they identify themselves for the purposes of the survey and for future reference by means of a surname.

This is why the *Domesday Book*, although written in Latin as was the practice for several centuries with both civic and ecclesiastical records, is an invaluable source for the early appearance of a wide range of English surnames.

Several of these names were coined in connection with occupations.

These include Baker and Smith, while Cooks, Chamberlains, Constables and Porters were to be found carrying out duties in large medieval households.

The church's influence can be found in names such as Bishop, Friar and Monk while the popular name of Bennett derives from the late fifth to mid-sixth century Saint Benedict, founder of the Benedictine order of monks.

The early medical profession is represented by Barber, while businessmen produced names that include Merchant and Sellers.

Down at the village watermill, the names that cropped up included Millar/Miller, Walker and Fuller, while other self-explanatory trades included Cooper, Tailor, Mason and Wright.

Even the scenery was utilised as in Moor, Hill, Wood and Forrest – while the hunt and the chase supplied names that include Hunter, Falconer, Fowler and Fox.

Colours are also a source of popular surnames, as in Black, Brown, Gray/Grey, Green and White, and would have denoted the colour of the clothing the person habitually wore or, apart from the obvious exception of 'Green', one's hair colouring or even complexion.

The surname Red developed into Reid, while

Blue was rare and no-one wanted to be associated with yellow.

Rather self-important individuals took surnames that include Goodman and Wiseman, while physical attributes crept into surnames such as Small and Little.

Many families proudly boast the heraldic device known as a Coat of Arms, as featured on our front cover.

The central motif of the Coat of Arms would originally have been what was borne on the shield of a warrior to distinguish himself from others on the battlefield.

Not featured on the Coat of Arms, but highlighted on page three, is the family motto and related crest – with the latter frequently different from the central motif.

Adding further variety to the rich cultural heritage that is represented by surnames is the appearance in recent times in lists of the 100 most common names found in England of ones that include Khan, Patel and Singh – names that have proud roots in the vast sub-continent of India.

Echoes of a far distant past can still be found in our surnames and they can be borne with pride in commemoration of our forebears.

Chapter two:

Myth and legend

A name that has a resonance with England's legendary past, 'Robinson' derives from the medieval given name 'Robin', a diminutive of 'Robert.'

Stemming from the Anglo-Saxon 'hrothi' and 'berhta', meaning 'fame-bright', in the form of the forename 'Robin' it became popularised through both Robin Goodfellow, a mischievous character in poet and dramatist William Shakespeare's late sixteenth century play *Midsummer Night's Dream* and also through Robin of Locksley.

This was the semi-mythical outlaw who, along with his band of merry men, emerged from their stronghold in the depths of Sherwood Forest in Nottinghamshire to steal from the powerful rich to give to the oppressed poor.

Because of the name's ancient roots, it means that flowing through the veins of many bearers of the name today may well be the blood of those Germanic tribes who invaded and settled in the south and east of the island of Britain from about the early fifth century.

Known as the Anglo-Saxons, they were composed of the Jutes, from the area of the Jutland Peninsula in modern Denmark, the Saxons from Lower Saxony, in modern Germany and the Angles from the Angeln area of Germany.

It was the Angles who gave the name 'Engla land', or 'Aengla land' – better known as 'England.'

They held sway in what became England from approximately 550 to 1066, with the main kingdoms those of Sussex, Wessex, Northumbria, Mercia, Kent, East Anglia and Essex.

Whoever controlled the most powerful of these kingdoms was tacitly recognised as overall 'king' – one of the most noted being Alfred the Great, King of Wessex from 871 to 899.

It was during his reign that the famous *Anglo-Saxon Chronicle* was compiled – an invaluable source of Anglo-Saxon history – while Alfred was designated in early documents as *Rex Anglorum Saxonum*, King of the English Saxons.

Other important Anglo-Saxon works include the epic *Beowulf* and the seventh century *Caedmon's Hymn*.

Through the Anglo-Saxons, the language known as Old English developed, later transforming from the eleventh century into Middle English – sources from which many popular English surnames of today such as Robinson derive.

The Anglo-Saxons meanwhile, had usurped the power of the indigenous Britons – who referred to them as 'Saeson' or 'Saxones.'

It is from this that the Scottish Gaelic term for 'English people' of 'Sasannach' derives, the Irish Gaelic 'Sasanach' and the Welsh 'Saeson.'

We learn from the *Anglo-Saxon Chronicle* how the religion of the early Anglo-Saxons was one that pre-dated the establishment of Christianity in the British Isles.

Known as a form of Germanic paganism, with roots in Old Norse religion, it shared much in common with the Druidic 'nature-worshipping' religion of the indigenous Britons.

But the death knell of the Anglo-Saxons was sounded with the Norman Conquest of 1066, a date by which England had become a nation with several powerful competitors to the throne.

In what were extremely complex family, political and military machinations, the monarch was Harold II, who had succeeded to the throne following the death of Edward the Confessor.

But his right to the throne was contested by two powerful competitors – his brother-in-law King Harold Hardrada of Norway, in alliance with Tostig, Harold II's brother, and Duke William II of Normandy.

In what has become known as The Year of Three Battles, Hardrada invaded England and gained victory over the English king on September 20 at the battle of Fulford, in Yorkshire.

Five days later, however, Harold II decisively defeated his brother-in-law and brother at the battle of Stamford Bridge.

But he had little time to celebrate his victory, having to immediately march south from Yorkshire to encounter a mighty invasion force led by Duke William that had landed at Hastings, in East Sussex.

Harold's battle-hardened but exhausted force confronted the Normans on October 14, drawing up a strong defensive position, at the top of Senlac Hill, building a shield wall to repel William's cavalry and infantry.

The Normans suffered heavy losses, but through a combination of the deadly skill of their archers and the ferocious determination of their cavalry they eventually won the day.

Anglo-Saxon morale had collapsed on the

battlefield as word spread through the ranks that Harold, last of the Anglo-Saxon kings, had been killed.

William was declared King of England on December 25, and the complete subjugation of his Anglo-Saxon subjects followed.

Those Normans who had fought on his behalf were rewarded with the lands of Anglo-Saxons, many of whom sought exile abroad as mercenaries.

Within an astonishingly short space of time, Norman manners, customs and law were imposed on England – laying the basis for what subsequently became established 'English' custom and practice.

But beneath the surface, old Anglo-Saxon culture was not totally eradicated, with some aspects absorbed into those of the Normans, while faint echoes of the Anglo-Saxon past is still seen today in the form of popular surnames such as Robinson.

It is with Yorkshire that the Robinson name is particularly identified, with a John Richard Robinson recorded in Wakefield in 1324, although it first appears on official record, in the form of its popular spelling variant of 'Robins', in Cambridgeshire in 1273.

Subsequent bearers of the name came to stamp an indelible mark on the historical record.

In the early Robinson homeland of Yorkshire,

Thomas Robinson was the influential eighteenth century politician and diplomat who held high office and was rewarded by being elevated to the Peerage as 1st Baron Grantham.

Born in 1695, a son of Sir William Robinson, of Newby-on-Swale, Member of Parliament (MP) for York from 1697 to 1772, he served as English Ambassador to Austria from 1730 to 1748.

Serving as MP for Christchurch from 1749 to 1761 and for a time Leader of the House of Commons, before his death in 1770 he also served as Postmaster-General.

His son Thomas Robinson, 2nd Baron Grantham, born in 1738, also served for a time as MP for Christchurch while from 1771 to 1779 he served as Ambassador to Spain.

Also entrusted with other high offices that included President of the Board of Trade and, from 1782 to 1783, Foreign Secretary, he died in 1786.

One particularly poignant tale concerning bearers of the Robinson name relates to Mary Robinson, better known to posterity as "The Maid of Buttermere."

Born in 1778 in Buttermere, in the rolling and rugged splendour of England's Lake District, it was in 1802 that the local beauty, shepherdess and daughter of the village's Fish Inn married a gentleman known as Colonel Hope.

But it transpired that the charming and smooth-talking 'Colonel Hope', who claimed to be the brother of an earl, was an already-married forger and fraudster by the name of John Hatfield.

He was exposed shortly after his bigamous marriage to the unwitting Mary and was arrested.

Hatfield managed to escape but, captured a few months later, was hanged in Carlisle after being found guilty of a string of forgery offences.

Public subscriptions were raised on behalf of the romantically-cheated Mary Robinson who, in 1807, finally found true love when she married a local farmer with whom she had four children.

She died in 1837 and was buried in the churchyard of St Kentigern's at Calbeck, while she is mentioned in William Wordsworth's poem *The Prelude* and is also the subject of the 1987 Melvyn Bragg novel *The Maid of Buttermere*.

Chapter three:

Battle honours

Bearers of the Robinson name have gained high honours and distinction on the bloody fields of conflict.

Born to English parents in India in 1895, Leefe Robinson was a recipient during the First World War of the Victoria Cross (VC), the highest award for valour in the face of enemy action for British and Commonwealth forces.

It had been on the night of 2/3 September of 1916 that Lieutenant Robinson, piloting a B.E. 2c night fighter over Cuffley, Hertfordshire, shot down one of 16 German airships that had launched a massive bombing raid over England.

Raked by Robinson's machine-gun fire, the airship fell to earth in flames killing all its crew.

The action had been watched by thousands of Londoners who, in true patriotic fashion, cheered the British pilot's aerial feat of arms and sang the National Anthem.

The first British pilot to shoot down a German airship over Britain during the First World

War and the first person to be awarded the VC for bravery in action in the United Kingdom, Robinson was later shot down over the Western Front in April of 1917.

Captured and imprisoned in Germany, he made several unsuccessful escape attempts and died about a month after the conflict ended in November 1918 from the effects of the Spanish flu epidemic.

There is a memorial to him near the spot in Hertfordshire where the airship crashed.

Also in the air, Basil Robinson was a noted British bomber pilot of the Second World War.

Born in 1912 in Gateshead, Tyne and Wear, he was involved in No. 35 Squadron's air raid in December of 1941 on the German battleships *Gneisenau* and *Scharnhorst* – an action for which he was awarded the Distinguished Flying Cross (DFC).

Promoted to commander of 35 Squadron, it was while returning from a raid over Turin, Italy on the night of 18/19 November 1942 that a target indicator flare burst into flames in the bomb bay of his Hanley Page Halifax bomber.

With the flames set to trigger an explosion in the bomb bay, Robinson ordered his six fellow crewmen to bail out, maintaining a level flight to allow them to do so.

The flames eventually died out, and Robinson was able to single-handedly pilot the aircraft back to a British airfield.

Later promoted to Group Captain, he was killed in August of 1943 when his bomber was shot down during a raid on Berlin.

It was as a geographer and cartographer that Arthur H. Robinson performed valuable service during the Second World War.

Born in 1915 to American parents in Montreal, Canada, he served during the war as director of the map division of America's Office of Strategic Services (OSS) – forerunner of the Central Intelligence Agency (CIA) – and as Chief of the U.S. Map Office.

It was under his direction that thousands of hand-drawn maps of Europe were produced – all vital to the Allied war effort.

Awarded the Legion of Merit by the United States Army for his contribution, he later served as professor of the geography department of the University of Wisconsin.

The university's map library is named in his

honour, while he also served as president of both the International Cartographic Association and the Association of American Geographers; he died in 2004.

Bearers of the Robinson name have also made their mark in the often cut-throat world of politics.

Instrumental in the foundation of the International Criminal Court, Arthur Napoleon Raymond Robinson, better known as A.N.R. Robinson, is the politician who also served from 1997 to 2003 as 3rd President of his native Trinidad and Tobago.

Born in 1926, it was while serving from 1986 to 1991 as the nation's 3rd Prime Minister that he put forward the proposal during the 44th Session of the U.N. General Assembly for the creation of a permanent international court to deal with the scourge of the world-wide drug trade.

His proposal was finally put into effect with the inauguration in 2002 of the International Criminal Court – which is also charged with hearing cases of crimes against humanity.

It was in recognition of his services to not only his own nation but also to the community of nations in general that the country's airport in Tobago was in 2011 renamed the A.N.R. Robinson International Airport.

Bearers of the Robinson name have also been prominent in the politics of both the Republic of Ireland and Northern Ireland.

Born Mary Bourke in Ballina, Co. Mayo, in 1944 but better known by her married name, Mary Robinson is the distinguished Irish former politician who served from 1990 to 1997 as the first female President of the Republic of Ireland.

An academic and barrister, she served as a member of the Irish Senate from 1969 to 1989, while in the international arena she served from 1997 to 2002 as the United Nations High Commissioner for Human Rights.

Her many honours and awards include the 2004 Amnesty International Ambassador of Conscience Award, while in 2009 she was awarded the Presidential Medal of Freedom – the United States' highest civilian award.

In Northern Irish politics, Peter Robinson was, as leader of the Democratic Unionist Party (DUP), elected First Minister of Northern Ireland in June of 2008.

Born in Belfast in 1948, in 1979, he was elected to the British House of Commons for the Belfast East constituency.

Married to the former DUP politician Iris Robinson, born Iris Collins in Belfast in 1949, he had to temporarily stand down from his position as First Minister in early 2000 following allegations concerning his wife's personal affairs.

First Lady of the United States since her husband's election as President in November of 2008, Michelle LaVaughn Robinson is better known as Michelle Obama.

Born in Chicago in 1964, the daughter of a city water plant employee and local Democratic Party activist, it was while working with a Chicago law firm that she met her future husband.

Chapter four:

On the world stage

A major star of Hollywood's Golden Age, Emanuel Goldenberg was the American actor better known as Edward G. Robinson. Born in 1893 in Bucharest, Romania, he was aged 10 when he arrived with his parents in New York, later receiving a scholarship to the city's American Academy of Dramatic Arts.

Changing his name to the one by which he would become famous, with the 'G' standing for 'Goldenberg', he rose to fame with film roles that include that of Rico in the 1931 *Little Caesar* and Rocco in the 1948 *Key Largo*. Other major film credits include the 1937 *The Last Gangster*, the 1944 *Double Indemnity*, the 1965 *The Cincinnati Kid* and, in the year of his death in 1973, *Soylent Green*.

Inducted into the American Film Institute's list of the 25 greatest male stars in American cinema, he was also posthumously honoured with an Honorary Academy Award for his work in the film industry.

Best known for his role as Professor Bernard

Quatermass in the 1955 BBC television serial *Quatermass II*, **John Robinson** was the English actor born in Liverpool in 1908.

Film credits include the 1936 *The Scarab*, while his final role was five years before his death in 1979 in the television series *Fall of Eagles*.

An actor of stage, television and film, **Andy Robinson** was born in 1942 in New York City.

Best known for his role as the serial killer Scorpio in the 1971 film *Dirty Harry*, starring Clint Eastwood, other film credits include the 2005 *A Question of Loyalty*, while he also had the role from 1993 to 1999 of Edim Garak on the television series *Star Trek: Deep Space Nine*.

A journalist and author in addition to radio and television presenter, **Robert Robinson** was born in 1927 in Liverpool.

Beginning work on British television in the mid-1950s as a journalist, he later presented popular series throughout the 1960s and 1970s that included *Open House*, *Points of View*, *Take it or Leave It* and *Ask the Family*.

He died in 2011, after having also presented BBC radio shows that include *Stop the Week* and BBC Radio 4's flagship *Today* programme.

Also on British television screens, **Tony Robinson** is the actor, comedian, broadcaster, author and political campaigner born in 1946 in Homerton, London.

Known for his role as Baldrick in the television comedy series *Blackadder* and as presenter of the *Time Team* archaeology series, he is also a campaigner on behalf of the Labour Party, while in 2013 he was knighted in recognition of his services to British entertainment.

Nicknamed the "Queen of Mean" for her acerbic role as the hostess of the popular BBC Television game show *The Weakest Link*, **Anne Robinson** is the journalist and television presenter born in 1944 in Crosby, Merseyside.

Also a presenter on the BBC consumer affairs programme *Watchdog*, her 2001 autobiography, *Memoirs of an Unfit Mother*, describes her former battle with alcohol.

Behind the camera lens, **David Robinson**, born in 1930 in Lincoln, is the British film critic and author whose books include his 1968 *Hollywood in the Twenties*.

Born in London in 1977, **Zuleikha Robinson** is the British-American actress best known for her role as Ilana in the American television series *Lost*, while film credits include the 2000 *Timecode* and, from 2007, *The Namesake*.

She is a sister of the field botanist and taxonomist **Dr Alistair Robinson**, born in 1980, whose specialisms include ecology and conservation biology.

Also in the sciences, **Sir Robert Robinson** was the English organic chemist who won the Nobel Prize for Chemistry in 1947 for his research on plant dyestuffs.

Born in 1886 in Chesterfield, Derbyshire, he was appointed the first professor of pure and applied chemistry at the University of Sydney in 1912 and later appointed a fellow of Magdalen College, Oxford.

Inventor of the symbol for benzene while working at the University of St Andrews in 1923, he is also known for inventing the use of the 'curly arrow' to represent electron motion.

Also the discoverer of the molecular structures of morphine and penicillin, he died in 1975.

In chemistry of a rather different nature, **Frank Mason Robinson**, born in 1845 in Corinth, Maine, and later settling in Atlanta, Georgia, had been a humble secretary and bookkeeper for the Pemberton Chemical Company when, in 1886, he created the name 'Coca-Cola.'

His boss, Dr John Pemberton, had been experimenting with a formula for a soft drink using cola leaves, kola nuts and other ingredients.

Satisfied with the outcome, he asked Robinson to think of a name – and what is now the internationally recognised brand name of Coca-Cola was born.

In addition to naming the drink, Robinson was also responsible for the distinct script, known as Spenserian, in which the name Coca-Cola appears.

Pemberton first introduced his new drink at the Jacobs Pharmacy in Atlanta in 1886, later selling the formula to Asa G. Chandler.

Chandler took Robinson on as secretary and treasurer of his company – giving him responsibility for the first major advertising of Coca-Cola. Later appointed a company director he died, a very wealthy man, in 1924.

Another bearer of the Robinson name with a particularly inventive turn of mind is the American engineer **Franklin D. Robinson**, born in 1930 on Whidbey Island, Washington D.C.

Designer in the early 1970s of the Robinson R22 helicopter, he is a recipient of the Howard Hughes Memorial Award from the Southern California Aeronautic Association.

A pioneer in advertising and opinion survey research, **Claude E. Robinson**, along with George Gallup, was instrumental in the setting up of what are now known as Gallup Polls.

Born in 1900 in Portland, Oregon, it was in 1948 that, along with Gallup, he founded the advertising research company Gallup and Robinson; he died in 1961.

Bearers of the Robinson name have also achieved fame in the world of music.

The recipient of a Grammy Lifetime Achievement Award in 1999 and, in 2002, America's National Medal of Arts, William Robinson is the rhythm and blues singer, songwriter and producer better known as **Smokey Robinson**.

Dubbed "King of Motown" and best known for his association with the band The Miracles, whose hits include the 1970 *The Tears of a Clown*, he is also a successful solo artist.

Born in 1940 in Detroit, he was inducted into the Rock and Roll Hall of Fame in 1987.

Recipient of a Grammy Lifetime Achievement Award in 1987, Ray Charles Robinson was the American soul, rhythm and blues and gospel musician better known by his shortened, stage name of **Ray Charles**.

Described by Frank Sinatra as "the only true genius in show business", he was born into a poor background in Albany, Georgia, in 1930.

Starting to lose his sight at the age of five, he went completely blind two years later. It was while attending a school for the deaf and blind from 1937 to 1945 that he developed what would blossom into a great musical talent.

Playing in bands as a teenager, his fist hit was with the Maxin Trio in 1949 with *Confession Blues*.

A string of solo hits followed, including the 1963 *Take These Chains From My Heart* and the 1967 *Here We Go Again*, while his version of *Georgia on My Mind* was adopted as the state song of Georgia in 1979.

Also a recipient of a star on the Hollywood Walk of Fame, he died in 2004.

In contemporary music, **Tom Robinson**, born in 1950 in Cambridge, is the English singer and songwriter and gay rights activist who enjoyed hits with his Tom Robinson Band that include *Glad to be Gay* and *2-4-6-8 Motorway*.

Beginning his career as a busker at the tender age of six, **Bill "Bojangles" Robinson** was the American tap dancer and actor born in 1878 in Richmond, Virginia.

Best known for dancing with child star Shirley Temple in a number of films of the 1930s, his credits include the 1934 *The Little Colonel* and, from 1935, *The Littlest Rebel*.

He died in 1949, while there is a statue of him in his hometown of Richmond – and May 25th, the date of his birth, is officially recognised in his honour in the U.S.A. as "National Tap Dance Day."

From music to sport, Walker Smith Jr. was the American world boxing champion better known as **Sugar Ray Robinson**.

Born in 1921 in Ailey, Georgia, the son of a corn, cotton and peanut farmer, his professional boxing debut was in 1940 – the first of 200 fights in which he would have 173 wins, 108 of these by knock-out.

Holder of the World Welterweight title from 1946 to 1951 and the World Middleweight title in 1951, he retired in 1952 only to return later and take the middleweight title again in 1955.

When his boxing career did finally end, he attempted a career as an entertainer – but with little success.

He died, in poverty, in 1989. Regarded as one of the greatest boxers of all time and an inductee of the International Boxing Hall of Fame, he was featured on a commemorative U.S. postage stamp in 2006.

Also in the boxing ring, **Steve Robinson**, born in Cardiff in 1968, is the Welsh retired boxer who held the World Featherweight Champion title from April 1993 to September 1995.

On the rugby pitch, **Andy Robinson**, born in 1964 in Taunton, Somerset, is the retired rugby union player who played for the England national team from 1988 to 1995 and who was appointed head coach of the Scotland national team in June of 2009.

In the creative world of the written word, **Edwin Robinson**, born in 1869 in Lincoln County, Maine, and who died in 1935, was the American poet who won no fewer than three Pulitzer Prizes for his work.

These were for 1922 *Collected Poems*, the 1925 *The Man Who Died Twice* and the 1928 *Tristram*.

One Robinson whose name has entered everyday language was William Heath Robinson, better known as **W. Heath Robinson**.

Born in 1872 in Islington, London, the cartoonist and illustrator became known for his drawings of complex and eccentric machines and contraptions.

So famous did these weird and wonderful drawings become that 'Heath Robinson', even before the illustrator's death in 1944, had entered the lexicon as 'a description of any unnecessary complex and implausible contraption.'